THE GRACE TO GRIEVE:

Finding God's Grace and Provision in

Unexpected Places

By Kiya Ward Shears

The Grace to Grieve: Finding God's Grace and
Provision in Unexpected Places

For Mommy and Daddy who taught me to articulate my thoughts, give voice to the voiceless and cherish my God-given life. To George, my incredible husband, I love you.

Table of Contents:

Forward

This is a story of what happens when the worst thing happens—in this case, a young woman who loses her mother and her father in quick succession before she reaches the age of thirty—and of the process of re-membering the very human details of illness, death, grief, and hope.

This is a story of having to grow up, to give up the illusory nature of achievement, success and expectations of others in order to be one's true self.

This is a story of the ways that grief is particular to every person, just as each of us is created particularly in the image of God. There is no right or wrong way to grieve, but Kiya's memoir of her own specific circumstances offers wisdom for all of us.

This is, finally, a story of resurrection life, for those who have died, as Christian faith promises us, but also for the living who mourn but go on living.

As scripture tells us, God's mercies are new every morning, so every day we make a new beginning.

My hope and prayer for all of you who read Kiya's book is that you will recognize some part of your own human journey in her story, and that you will be offered the gifts of honest reckoning, compassion, humor and love in the telling of it. For you who need it, may you find the grace to grieve.

Blessings and peace.

The Reverend Ellen Echols Purdum
Assistant Dean of Student Life and Spiritual Formation
Candler School of Theology, Emory University

CHAPTER 1:

Permission

I am patient when waiting in a long line at the grocery store. I am patient when my seven-year-old bonus son has an entire monologue about his eating preferences for the day. I am patient when someone abruptly cuts me off in Atlanta traffic. I am patient when a family of deer come inches from taking out my headlights in North Carolina. I am patient in helping others navigate their trials. I am patient as I lift prayers and climb through Scripture, literature, and biblical commentaries to exegete a biblical text. I can be very patient, but I've found that I lack patience in my grieving process.

It's been three years since my parents transitioned, yet there are still days when I experience the lowest of lows; days when I feel completely lethargic and want nothing more than to curl in the fetal position and scream for them. It is the low points that leave me perplexed and distraught, for surely, I should have learned how to cope with loss by now, right?

As a self-proclaimed "over-achiever" I find the grieving process exhausting and time-consuming. I'm not fond of crying, so embracing my tears is another matter in and of itself. Furthermore, making sense of such great and traumatic loss isn't something that comes overnight, for I am 31 years old and both of my parents are dead. That truth alone is a mouth-full that I still struggle to embrace some days; it's a truth that leaves an unrelatable stench in most interactions. The truth of the matter is that I don't enjoy the grieving process (at all), yet when I seek God on the matter, He always reminds me of His "grace."

I once heard grace described as "unmerited favor from God." However, I never considered grace in terms of grief until a mentor, Ellen Echols Purdum, sternly said to me, "Kiya, you must give yourself the grace to grieve!" Raising my hopeless and tear-filled eyes from my lowered head, our gaze locked as Ellen continued, "...you must give yourself permission to feel the way you feel; to experience the fullness of this process." As silly as it may sound, I'd never thought of grieving in that way. I am a "Type A" person, thus the idea of a "process" not having a chronological order didn't exactly bring me comfort. Yet, giving myself the *grace to grieve* has been the fuel to my everyday functionality.

Again, I once heard grace defined as "unmerited favor from God." I don't know who coined the definition, but I do know that putting the word "grace" and "grieving" in the same sentence is an oxymoron in and of itself. There is nothing about crying throughout the night that feels like favor;

there is nothing about watching a loved one's casket lowered into the ground that feels like favor; there is nothing about the agonizing heart-ache of losing a loved one that feels remotely like favor. Yet, it's there. God's grace, His unmerited favor, is threaded throughout the grieving process; God grants His sons and daughters with the *grace to grieve.*

Giving myself the *grace to grieve* isn't always lingering on fond memories or clutching the pearls Mom gifted me our last Christmas together. Instead, giving myself the *grace to grieve* is holding onto the uncertainty of each day; it is constantly telling Jesus how much I need Him on this journey; it's crying to experience a God who wipes my tears; it's not "faking" energy when I really don't have it; it's being frustrated with God's will without feeling like a hypocrite; it's sitting quietly with no words to say, knowing that Jesus is interceding on my behalf. This type of grace gives me permission to be impatient with myself, yet the ability to forgive my impatience with God.

Giving myself the *grace to grieve* is an everyday process. Yet, in this process, I'm also learning about grace in other areas of my life: the grace to forgive quicker, the grace to grow stronger, the grace to unapologetically "be", the grace to move forward without knowing every detail of God's plan for my life; and the grace to find my words in what feels like a season of muted prayers. Each chapter included in this book is a part of my personal grieving process that led me to experience God's grace. It is my prayer that through this book, you are led to experience God's grace in your own grieving process; I pray that through my voice you find a voice to your own hurt that leads you closer to Christ.

CHAPTER 2:

Grown

I, like most adolescents, spent my youth aspiring to be "grown." I lived for dressing up, thinking for myself and being as independent as possible (under the guise of Mommy, of course). As I matriculated through life, endless opportunities encouraged my independence and led me to feel as if there was nothing that I could not achieve. Admittance into my top choice schools, being voted as the Homecoming Queen at my undergraduate university and always being the one chosen for leadership opportunities left me indestructible. Throughout each of these seasons of cultivated success, Mom and Dad provided support and nourishment. The support ranged from paying application fees, proofreading papers (Thanks Mom!) and showing up on time for awards ceremonies. Not to mention there were endless prayers and intercession made on my behalf by my parents who I truly believe thought I could accomplish anything. It is hard for me to find the words to explain the joy and pride of having a support system who constantly poured into me, pushed me to take risks and promised never to leave me alone. To put it plainly, the support of my parents made me feel covered, protected and invincible. If I could think it, it was achievable no matter the apparent barriers or competition at hand.

Yet, no matter how high my heels or numerous my titles, my parents had a way of releasing the *little girl* inside of me. Around them, I wasn't "Minister Kiya" or "Kiya Ward, B.A., M.A." I was simply their "baby." In fulfillment of that role, as their certified "baby", I would sit on my mom's lap ("Girl, you are going to break my legs," she would say), daydream in the den with Mom about the future of my ministry, and go grocery shopping in their kitchen (their food tasted better). I am convinced that Mom bought extra groceries just to make sure I always had bags full of goodies when leaving home. This generosity was not limited to me as their baby, just ask any of my friends who will laugh as they reflect on the many times Mom would insist on them taking a bottle of Welch's Sparkling Grape Juice or a to-go plate. In that atmosphere of giving time, resources and attention, it was easy for my world to make sense with my parents. Truthfully, with Mommy and Daddy, I didn't have to be a day older than being their "baby."

Upon my parents' death, all of that changed or as I would say, it came crashing down uncontrollably. It felt as if I'd been thrust from my unmovable throne as their "baby" into an abandoned reality; a reality that lacked a "safe space." The jolt of being forced into this new reality was heartbreaking and painful to navigate. Not to mention, that feeling of being covered and protected was gone. I felt numb, abandoned and powerless. Something as simple as being able to call Mom to discuss a challenging situation or having Dad fix something, was completely out of my grasp. I'd lived my entire life with the excitement of being independent, just to come to a place where all I wanted was to depend on my parents. It was uncomfortable. It was lonely. I desperately yearned for normality with my parents. I wanted Dad to tell me about the weather for the next five days and I longed for Mom to ask me if I'd been eating in the midst of my busy schedule; I craved to hear Dad ask if I was still "making A's" and for Mom to tell me how proud she was of my newest ministry project; I wanted Dad to declare that my heels were too high and for Mom to ask if I wanted to run with her to DSW because they were having a weekend sale. For once in my life, I didn't want to be *grown*... all I wanted was to be their "baby" again.

CHAPTER 3:

Seventeen

I'm not superstitious and have never really had a "favorite" or meaningful number until my parents died. Anyone who has experienced loss will tell you that you don't forget the day your life changes forever. You remember where you were physically when you found out the news, you remember the pain and you remember the weight of death. It's almost like your senses go into overdrive as they commit the pain to memory. So, it goes without saying that my mother dying on the 17th was significant.

It was August 17th, 2016 at 4:05pm when I stood over my mother's comatose body as she took her last breath at the age of 65. I remember the motionless look on her face; the thick glare in her eyes; and the still smell of the room. Her arms laid straight beside her, her hands with a slight bend and her breathing was unsteady. In an unexpected shift of emotions, the more unsteady her breathing became, the more accepting I became of her unavoidable exit. "It's ok, Mommy," I said, "I love you Mommy. You can go. Everything is going to be OK," I told her with an assurance that I'm not even sure how I mustered. This confidence was in total contrast to the screaming I'd done in the hallways an hour earlier; the nervous quivering that overtook me as I responded to the doctor's question, "Would you like your mother resuscitated?"

I was a certified "Momma's Baby," who in a matter of seconds became the woman my mother raised me to be. Closing the estate, taking care of my father, balancing my own jobs, and going to school full time became my regimen. Atlanta during the week and North Carolina on weekends was my weekly itinerary, but in a weird, very Type-A kind of way, staying busy was my therapy. I had to keep pushing because there was business to be taken care of and I had a father who depended on me greatly. The busier I was, the less time I had to focus on the loss; the busier I was, the more forced I felt to get out of bed each morning. No matter how big or small, each day I had to find a reason to get up; a reason to live.

As my regimen became familiar, I was again faced with an unexpected jolt. It was December 11th, 2016 at 3:45am when I got the call that my father passed at Hospice. I'd left him just three hours prior as I told the nurse, "I can't take this, I can't just wait for him to die." Watching Dad gasp for each breath as his skeleton of a body tried to keep up with the course rhythm of his breathing, was painful to watch. It was scary to watch. So, I stood by his bed, gave him a final look and said

"Goodnight." I also apologized for the years I'd mistook his tough love for lacking love; I apologized for the teen years that lingered into my twenties; I apologized for not understanding his frustrations that manifested in what I took to be harsh arguments with Mom and misappropriated anger. I thanked him for the four months prior in which I'd gotten to know him. Yes, he'd always been there physically, but I'd never taken the time to know Dad. I just saw him as an angry person with whom it was easier to walk on egg shells than get to know.

As I prepared to leave his bedside, there was a part of me that knew it was the last time I would see him; I knew it was the last time I would hear him breathing. I also knew that my father was not going to make the transition with anyone around, not even me. He was a "manly man" and a "proud" man. We'd been through a lot together in the weeks and months prior, but this last move was one he'd have to make without me.

Less than three hours later, I received the call. "Kiya, this is Jenny from Hospice," she said in a sure tone, "Your dad passed five minutes ago at 3:40am." Although his death was anticipated, it still hit me like a punch in the stomach. My heart raced out of my chest and I laid there staring at the ceiling. Part of me hoped I was dreaming, but I knew I was wide awake. Ironically enough, tears did not come nor did I scream, I simply turned on my lamp and I sat there...for hours I sat there just as I'd sat 17 weeks prior trying to make sense of God's plan.

In the days, weeks and months following their deaths, I was desperate to find meaning and purpose in the loss of Mom and Dad. Why did they die so young? Why did they die so close together?

Why did such a traumatic loss happen in my life? The truth is, ever since Mom died, I'd asked God *why*? I'd become enamored with understanding the fullness of what I was facing. I prayed for them to live, yet they both died. I longed for them, they seemed so far away. Yet, within the two months after Dad passed, there was a shift in my thinking. Suddenly, there was a shift in the core of my *why*. Instead of focusing on *why* my parents died, I started focusing on *why* God kept me through it all. There are people who literally "lose it" after the death of one parent. Yet there I was facing the loss of two parents in such a short period of time and I was still functioning; I was still believing.

It was in exploring the *why* of my provision that I began embracing the truth that God had a greater plan and purpose for my life. The way I see it, if God kept me through the tragedy of loss, surely, He had a greater plan and purpose for my life. I could spend the rest of my life asking God *why* He took my parents, but how much more encouraging is it to ask *why* He is keeping me. Surely God has something up His sleeve. If God didn't have a plan for me, the Funeral Director would have buried me right next to my parents. However, since God still has a plan for my life, I couldn't die even at the most vulnerable time of my life...and neither can you.

CHAPTER 4:

Love Lifted Me

My mother was the epitome of love. She adored the song "Love lifted me" as she used the old hymn title to reference times when she had to take the "high road" in tough situations; times when the enemy tried to bring her down and God's love brought her out. During the summer prior to her death, she started using this phrase more and more victoriously as she would declare, "Kiya, love lifted me!"

I spent the summer of 2016 as the interim pastor of a church in the Bahamas. It was one of the most exhilarating and informative experiences of my life. Yet, one of the most memorable parts of the excursion lied not on the beautiful island, but in the ongoing conversations I had with Mom. Mom loved hearing about the new foods I tried, the tiny crabs that always made their way under my front door and not to mention, the lizards which made themselves at home in my bedroom. She would laugh until tears filled her eyes, shoulders shaking uncontrollably as she nudged me for more details of each story. On Saturday nights, she'd attentively listen as I read her my sermon for the following day. "Oh Kiya," she'd say, "I love it!"

Throughout the summer, Mom constantly told me how much she enjoyed our conversations. She was a very complementary person, so her positive affirmation did not stand out to me; however, her solemn tone did. "Kiya," she would say, "I am going to miss this so much." Confused at her pessimism I would respond, "miss what?" "Talking with you like this" she would reply. Thinking that she was referring to how busy I would be when I returned to seminary in the fall I responded, "Oh Mommy, you know I always make time for you. Besides, I always call after my study groups and if I ever miss your call I always call back. It will be fine." Yet she would always respond so solemnly, "I will miss this."

In our summer conversations, Mom provided much insight and reiterated her love for our family. She would say, "Kiya, I love you so much" to which I would always say "Love you more" to which she would respond, "But you don't know how much I love you." It wasn't until I became a Bonus Mom, that I understood a fraction of what Mom meant.

On July 29th Mom had a flight booked with me and one of her closest friends to travel to New York City. I'd returned from the Bahamas only a day earlier and was confused at Mom's urgency to vacation. Mom was so adamant about this trip and I remember trying to convince her to push back our departure date. "Mom," I started, "Can we fly out next week? We could stay longer, or what if we wait until Labor Day or my fall break?" Yet Mom declined my pursuits and remained adamant about the timing (I'm so glad she did). The trip was very enjoyable as Mom had a bucket list of pre-planned activities, ranging from a visit to our favorite boutique in Manhattan, a pleasant stay at our favorite hotel and an exciting show on Broadway ("Motown The Musical"). Yet, our excursions didn't stop in the Big Apple.

Following our return from New York City, Mom traveled with me to Atlanta. During this trip we went to a recording of her favorite show, *Family Feud*. I will never forget the look of excitement on Mommy's face as we laughed, clapped and embraced the adventure. She was thrilled at the opportunity and we literally laughed together until it hurt. Only something did hurt. Mom was moving slower and had lost so much weight. The weight loss was actually the first thing I noticed the week prior when she picked me up from the airport. Her jaw line was more defined, her cheek bones lacking their natural plump appearance. She'd brushed off my questions of her health the week prior in New York, but I definitely knew something was wrong. She was constantly out of breath, which she blamed on allergies; there was a wound growing on her chest, which she attributed to a bug bite.

On commercial breaks, Steve Harvey told jokes and shared his testimony. Mom loved hearing how God moved in Steve's life; she loved hearing how God delivered him from so many "valley" experiences. Mom talked about Steve Harvey days after the recording. For our remaining time in Atlanta, we visited family, toured the city, and had lots of quality time at my apartment. In our quality time, she challenged me in areas of weakness and encouraged me to keep my faith despite adversity. By this time, I knew something was up and Mommy sensed every bit of my fear. "Kiya," she said while sitting on my green living room sofa, "I am not worried about me. I am worried about you worrying about me." How could I not worry? Something was wrong that, in my mind, Mom refused to address. As respectfully as I could, I'd interrogate her with health questions and wellness options until she'd shut down. "Kiya!" she'd exclaim, "That is enough."

We returned to North Carolina from Atlanta just one day prior to a retirement celebration given to Mom by her Bennett College family. After 26 years of serving Bennett College as a faculty member and administrator, she decided to retire on August 1, 2016. I remember asking Mommy what she could see herself doing one year after retirement to which she responded, "I will be teaching and writing." As I write this book, I can testify that mom is still teaching; that through this book, Mom is still writing.

The retirement celebration was blissful, yet solemn. Mom's colleagues seemed taken aback by her fragile frame and concerned with her shortness of breath. "Allergies" she said, "My allergies are acting up and have led to a few respiratory issues, so forgive my shortness of breath." Everyone knew Mom was a very private person, thus interrogating the "allergies" explanation would have been out of order. Mom's mysterious sickness was the "elephant in the room" that everyone tried to tip toe around with lighthearted stories and tears of laughter, "Oh, Dr. Ward, don't you remember..." or

"Dr. Ward, that time in..." and "Dr. Ward, thank you so much for..." Person after person poured around our table until there was literally a line of people waiting to speak with Mommy. A few tried to catch my eye with concern, but I knew too well how to divert my attention. Mom engaged each person in the line with smiles, words of encouragement and humility from their well wishes. "Oh, thank you" she said with her meticulous grace.

Of the stories told that day, my favorite came from the lips of Mommy. Mom was a passionate and dynamic orator; thus, she gave what would be her final public speech at this retirement celebration. In the speech she challenged those in attendance to find their "inner peace and follow it," to which she was met with a standing ovation. As she often did, Mom smiled humbly, tucked in her lips and took her seat. As we exited the premises, for what would be Mom's final time, Mom smiled and said, "That went well."

Mom's retirement celebration was on a Thursday and she passed the following Wednesday. Looking back, I see that Mom had already found the inner peace spoken of in her speech. And it is that inner peace, that God ordained peace, that is keeping me and leading me on this journey.

The day before Mom died was as normal a Tuesday as I could have expected. I ran a few errands as I prepared to return to Atlanta to start my second year of seminary the following week. Meanwhile, Mom spent the morning cleaning the house. At one point, Mom called me into her room and asked "Kiya, will you please help me hang up these suits." One by one she unpacked her suitcase from our recent travels and handed me the suits she'd purchased in NYC. When she came across a teal-colored suit coat with grey dress pants she said, "This one is my favorite." I smiled and said "It is pretty" to which she responded, "Kiya, THIS one is my favorite." I caught the emphasis she placed on it, but didn't take it as more than her expressing strong admiration for a new suit.

Later that morning Mommy said, "I was going to go to the hospital today, but I have some business to take care of in Durham." She spoke of going to the hospital like you or I would talk of going to the gas station. But for me, it was music to my ears because it meant that Mom was finally acknowledging that something *was* wrong and she was willing to get help! As calmly and confidently as I could, I assured Mom that I'd take care of her business in Durham if she'd just let me take her to the hospital.

This hospital visit had been a long-time coming. I knew something was "off" I just couldn't put my finger on it. An open wound on her breast and shortness of breath were the obvious symptoms, but I knew it was more. Mom lived years with Congestive Heart Failure and a strong medical mistrust that stemmed from her uncle falling dead in a doctor's office. That incident, mixed with her own experiences that she deemed "unfair" made her incredibly critical of any medical professional. I remember accompanying Mom to a doctor's appointment as a teen. Mom's blood pressure was through the roof, exceeding 180/100. The doctor was frantic as Mom calmly said, "Oh, it's always like this." At that age, I didn't realize the serious nature behind high blood pressure and even if I had, Mom's adamancy about receiving healing from God instead of a doctor was nothing I could compete with.

Yet, on this particular day, Mom was willing to negotiate with me. Surprisingly, Mom bargained with me, saying that she would allow me to take her to the hospital if I would grease her scalp. "WHAT! Mommy, I don't mind, but not one is going to see your hair at the hospital. We are only going to be there a day or two." "Kiya," she said sternly, "I would like you to grease my scalp." Greasing one's scalp is the process of parting the hair in different sections and putting oil or grease on the scalp. To me, this request was in terrible timing, we needed to get to the hospital. Confused and annoyed at the random nature of this request, I did as I was told as she sat peacefully. "Kiya," she began, "You are happy I'm going to the hospital, aren't you?" "YES," I responded emphatically, "Now you can get the help you need!" To which she responded, "I know how you feel. I felt that way with Mother." I don't know why she said that and I don't recall the next words of our conversation, for my focus was on greasing her scalp and figuring out how to braid her hair that would be covered by her wig. For the record, I don't braid hair and I don't remember ever greasing mom's scalp. To me, we were losing precious time, but if it would get her to the hospital, I was willing to do it.

It was years after Mom died that the revelation of greasing Mom's scalp gained significance. In Matthew 26:6-13, Mary anointed the feet of Jesus with expensive ointment from her alabaster box. As onlookers judged, Jesus responded in verse 12 by saying, "In pouring this ointment on my body, she has done it to prepare me for burial." Mom died within the 24 hours of me greasing her scalp; within 24 hours of me putting the oil on her. Could it be that the ointment used that day, was a last rite of sorts; could it be that without even knowing it, I was preparing Mom for death?

When I finished greasing Mom's scalp, she jokingly said "Now, let me go look in the mirror to see what you have done!" I suppose Mom approved of my impromptu handiwork because when she came back into the room, she was ready to go.

"Ok," She said as she took a seat, "Let me catch my breath." Our immediate family stood around her and held hands as we each said a prayer as we'd done so many times before. We prayed for healing, a speedy recovery and a quick return home. It was almost as if we were praying that God would take away a cold or something. Our prayers were meaningful, but short and to the point. Yet, there was something about the way Mom looked when she stood up. I can't fully describe it, but just as she'd done at Bennett the week prior, she raised her eyebrows, tucked in her lips and headed toward my car on the other side of the front door.

It took only moments for Mom to be admitted into the hospital from the ER on August 16th. Something weird happened as Mom, all of a sudden, began breathing heavily, "Give me an IV, I NEED AN IV. I'm so hot. I just need the fluids!" Her demand was aggressive and her tone was fierce and for the first time in my life, it looked like Mom was out of control. "One moment Dr. Ward, we just have to take..." The nurses bargained with Mom, but none of us were prepared for what would be revealed as they took off her yellow sleeveless top. "OH MY

GOD!" The nurse exclaimed running out of the room. A crowd of doctors soon filled the room as the "C" word began being thrown around. They needed to do a biopsy to confirm the diagnosis, but it was evident. The cancer, that "bug bite," had actually destroyed all the tissue on Mom's breasts. My eyes were met with raw whitish pink skin where her plump breast had once perched. Her skin on both breasts had literally rotted as one doctor said "I can literally see through your chest, Dr. Ward."

I knew the diagnosis was grim, but I was on the opposite spectrum of Mom in that I had full and complete trust in the doctors. A double mastectomy, so what! She'd get it and then we'd go on with our lives, only it wasn't that easy. "This is serious! Do you understand how sick your mother is?" I tried to stay strong as the next doctor came in and said "I'd give her six months to live." Wait, who said anything about her dying? She can't die or be that close to death, it's my Mommy; it's MY Mommy.

As hot aggressive tears streamed down my face, Mommy looked at me and said "Kiya, don't you worry about those doctors. Only God knows when I am going to go. Everything is going to be ok," "but Mommy," I cried, "You can't die; I can't make it without you." "Yes, you can," she replied, "You are stronger than you think. This will make you a better pastor." Tears continued to fall aimlessly as I excused myself from the room. Mom hated seeing me cry and I knew that listening to pessimistic reports would not ease my fear. I stood outside of the room for about five minutes as they dressed her massive "wound" after which I returned with a dry face, a smile to hide my fear and a bit of disbelief. From my purview, Mommy knew everything so if she said "only God knew" her timing, surely the doctors were wrong.

As doctors filtered in and out to observe her symptoms the re-occurring question was, "Why did you not come sooner?" after which they'd turn to me and ask "WHY DIDN'T YOU BRING HER SOONER?" It's a valid question, but one that only the child of someone with medical mistrust truly knows that pain of answering. If it were as easy as just bringing her to the doctor, don't they think I would have done that? Sure, they see her now, but what they didn't see was the nights I'd argued with Mom about her health; the times that I'd printed out health documents for her to read; the computer searches in which I found specialists at Duke Hospital and even UNC; the times I tried to convince her to show me the wound, but she'd refused; the pool of blood I'd found on her sheets that she refused to acknowledge; the doctors couldn't see the endless tears of frustration and fear that had accompanied me long before we got to that hospital room. No, I didn't know how bad it was, but I knew it was bad. Yet, the truth is that when an adult in their right mind is paralyzed by medical mistrust, not even their closest loved ones can release a sensation that "makes" them get help. No matter how many people declare how they would have changed the narrative, the truth is the only one in control of it is the one responsible for their own health. In the weeks following Mom's death, I had to overcome the insensitive comments by well-wishers who'd say, "I just wish you'd gotten her help sooner" or "I just wish I could have spoken with her; I could have gotten her to get help." With a still smile and an invisible knife cutting with their false optimism, I learned to leave those conversations untouched.

The weeks and months that followed Mom's death came with such a rush of emotions. If Mom loved me as much as she said she did, why would she leave me? My sadness turned to a bit of anger as I knew Mom's death was avoidable. If only she'd been willing to get help sooner.

One day while reconciling what felt to be the impossible question of why Mom didn't get help sooner, a dear family friend and Cancer Survivor by the name of Debra said, "Kiya, when faced with sickness we have a choice in how we die. Some people fight- they take every medicine, go through chemo and go to every appointment. Then, there are those who don't fight in the same way. Instead, they choose not to be poked and prodded for medical examining. Every person has a choice and your mother made her choice; Audrey chose to leave this world in her own way." It was the first time anyone had spoken to me about my mother in that way, but it made sense. As painful as it was truthful, Debra's words provided a type of closure for me that no amount of mental reckoning could. As the details of the weeks prior began to fall into place, it hit me that Mom's death wasn't random or unexpected. From the urgent trip to New York, the bucket list trip to Atlanta and even the greasing of her scalp, it was all a part of her plan...her plan to die.

Nostalgic memories of Mom greasing my grandmother's scalp on a Saturday afternoon linger in my mind as I think of greasing Mom's scalp that day she went to the hospital. I think of the beautiful teal-colored suit, which was the suit in which Mom was buried. I'd always focused on how much Mom didn't want to go to the hospital to get help, but I never focused on how Mom might have wanted to die. Perhaps because in my world, she would never die. And while her physical body died, her spirit lives on in the crease of my smile, the gaze of my almond colored eyes and in the precision of my work ethic. On days when I cry inconsolably, I hear her singing to me, "Momma's baby feel betta; Momma's baby feel betta, betta"; on days when I feel confused, I hear her wisdom; and on days when I want to give up, I feel her loving embrace. Song of Solomon 8:6 says that "love is as strong as death" and despite the numerous commentaries and concordances I've studied, this scripture has never held the weight it does now as I continue to feel Mom's love so present in my life.

To this day, I've found myself speechless at how a God who loves me so much, could take the one person in the world who I loved the most. The one thing that satisfies my deep inquiry is the realization that although I love Mommy, God loves her more. It was God's love that lifted my mommy three years ago and it is God's love that is keeping me three years   later.

CHAPTER 5:

The View

The only thing I dreaded more than Mom's funeral was the family viewing to approve her body the day before. I'd had the opportunity to avoid the viewing for my grandparents' burials years earlier, but I knew this was one "opportunity" I couldn't ignore. I arrived at the funeral home with my family and close friends early that Saturday morning. I was in a solemn mood; the last time I'd seen Mom she was being rolled under a dark sheet into the morgue of the hospital.

Everything about being at the funeral home felt wrong and awkward. As our family gathered outside of the chapel doors, we were greeted by the Funeral Director who asked if we were "ready." I don't remember saying "yes," but surely, I did because seconds later the white double doors to the Chapel opened, and just like that, my mother's body was in full *view*. I felt my heart drop to the pit of my stomach as my breath was simultaneously snatched from me. I turned to walk away from the doors. Tears streamed down my face for I knew it was going to be hard, but I just couldn't take that *view*. When I got myself together, my sister and I walked down the aisle and stood above my mother's body that was once so full of life. The room was silent and dimly lit with a small lamp that sat on the casket. "Her glasses, where are her glasses?" I asked. It was a meticulous request, but not having them would be just as bad as leaving the house without earrings. Without them, Mom appeared too vulnerable; naked. Quickly, her Burberry glasses were found and gently placed on her face. I tilted my head to the left, as I scanned Mom's dolled-up corpse.

I never knew how people could say the dead looked "good" until I saw my mother in that casket. She looked stunning. Her hair was perfect, glasses straightened, face perfectly plump and the shade of her melanin was perfect. What a relief it was to see Mom embody such beauty again, for in her final moments of life she looked so exhausted and frail. After the initial shock of seeing Mom in the casket, there was this silent sigh that hit the room. Family began chatting, with some even taking pictures. There was such a lite air in the room, which somehow traded the grave sadness for a moment of peace. The peace did not replace the pain of losing Mom, but just for a moment the peace provided the solace needed to get through the remainder of the viewing. Looking back, it is nothing but God's grace that got me through that viewing.

When the viewing hour was complete, I glanced at some of the casket pictures taken of Mom by family members. In looking at these pictures, there was something odd; something that truly stood out to me. None of the pictures looked like Mom. When looking into the casket, Mom looked just like herself. However, the smartphone pictures captured a different *view.* I kept looking back and forth between the casket and the pictures, but it just looked so different to me. The woman in the pictures was *not* my mom. To this day I often wonder why the pictures captured an image so different from what I saw with my own eyes. Perhaps the pictures made it look too "real" because while being present, I could simply pretend Mom was asleep; perhaps it's something I will never truly "get" or understand; perhaps the pictures simply captured a different *view.*

CHAPTER 6:

Muted Prayers

Praying for the living is something that's always come natural to me. Perhaps it's the "Now I lay me down to sleep" that was a part of my nightly routine as a kid or maybe it's the adult prayers for the prosperity and health of my loved ones. Whatever the root, praying for the living is easy or even exciting to me, which is why praying for my parents as they faced death felt like an oxymoron.

The first time I remember Mom praying was when I was maybe seven or eight years old. I recall walking into Mom's room as she knelt beside her bed. "Mommy!" I enthusiastically started. "Kiya," she said in a calm tone with her eyes still closed, "Mommy is praying." In the morning, at night and any time we were about to leave the house, Mommy would be on her knees praying. Sometimes I would innocently think she was sleeping as she would stay down there so long.

The last time I saw Mom on her knees praying was the Tuesday she had me take her to the hospital for what would be her final stay. I remember walking into her bedroom where she was knelt on the hardwood floors with her clasped hands propped up on the side of the bed. Later, when she exited her bedroom, my dad, brother and I met her in the living room as we joined hands in prayer.

The morning of what would be her last day on Earth, I woke up in the lounge chair beside her hospital bed. I didn't sleep well the night before and I don't think Mom did either. I literally woke up every hour of the night, each time finding Mom glancing over at me. Coming to terms with my lack of rest, I stood up and was met with great news- Mom wanted me to order her food. You must understand, Mom's eating had been fickle at best since I returned from the Bahamas. She'd ordered food and pick over it, barely putting the fork in her mouth. As you can imagine, I was ecstatic as Mom called out "fish, greens..." "Oh Mommy," I said, "You are making up for lost time today!" She smiled.

An Oncologist came in, then a Cardiac Nurse. Mom listened closely and when asked "Do you want help" she responded to the Oncologist saying, "Yes, I am ready to get help." It was a long time coming, but finally help was here and everything was working out better than planned. Soon, the room cleared out again. "Mommy," I began, "we haven't prayed together today." Holding hands, I prayed first and Mom's brief prayer followed. I had no idea that she would die hours later; I had no idea that would be the last time I'd hear Mommy pray. Moments later I pulled out my phone and started reading to her Psalm 100.

"Mommy," I said, "Psalm 100 was the first scripture you helped me memorize at Mount Sinai as a little girl." I got through maybe the first three verses when I realized that Mom wasn't making eye contact with me anymore. You must understand, Mom was very personable, so if someone was talking to her, she ensured devoted eye contact. "Mommy, is something wrong" I asked standing up and placing my phone to the side I took a closer look at Mom's eyes, which were now glazed over and fixed staring straight ahead. "Uh-huh" she grunted. Screaming, I ran out of the room and down the hall. "HELP! MY MOM NEEDS HELP!!! SHE WAS JUST TALKING TO ME, BUT NOW SHE CAN'T RESPOND! HELP!" Like a scene out of Grey's Anatomy, doctors and nurses rushed into the room with an array of medical chatter. Moments later we were in an elevator. "It's ok, Mommy. I'm right here," I assured her, hoping she could still hear me. She was in the MRI room only a matter of seconds before her stats dipped, leaving us in the ICU.

I vividly recall standing by my mother's comatose body in ICU saying aloud, "Mommy, it's ok for you to go. Everything is going to be ok...but Mom if this is one of those times where God is going to completely heal you and bring you back, that would be great! I don't want you to think I'm giving up on you." Similarly, I prayed daily with Dad in his final weeks and I'd always include, "... this is what the doctors are saying...but we know You, God, can change this entire situation."

Something about praying for my parents in their final weeks, days and hours made me feel as if I was doubting God. As I watched my father's organs fail, was it pessimistic for me to pray for a smooth transition? Did I administer last rites too soon? Was it too optimistic or even unrealistic for me to pray for his healing? At what point do prayers for "healing" and "restoration" become prayers of "peace" and "understanding"? I was never really sure if there was a "right" or "wrong" answer for the questions posed above, but I knew I could not go wrong praying, "Thy will be done." When I started praying for God's will, I could better understand that God held the present and the future of my parents; that He held their current life and their eternal life. For death, itself, was not a "finite" act, but a transition.

In 1 Corinthians 15:55, Paul says, "Where, O death, is your victory? Where, O death, is your sting?" Yet if we will be honest, the wording seems out of place doesn't it. For the truth is that death does sting, it is painful, uncomfortable and it aches. It has the makings of being stung by something indeed, doesn't it? The truth is, Paul in this text isn't encouraging believers not to cry or mourn; he isn't saying it won't be painful. Instead, in context, Paul is reminding us that the stinger of death is sin; but Christ, by dying on the cross, has taken out the stinger; he has made atonement for sin, he has obtained remission of it. You see, if Jesus had died never to rise again, it would have proved that death had power. Instead, when Jesus died on the cross Jesus looked death in the face. When He rose on the third day, He overcame death, and because Jesus overcame death, death has no power over us; death is not some finite thing that happens; it's not the end all be all; death isn't where our story ends.

Once I embraced this understanding, I prayed for my parents without the worry of being "right" or "wrong." I asked God for guidance on how exactly to pray and in response He only required my heart. Thus, my prayers in their final hours became worship. I sang to mom ("Glory, glory, hallelujah, since I laid my burdens down") and I encouraged Dad ("Everything is going to be ok; you are ok"). During my weary time, I found worship. Though I was only 28 years old when Mom died and 29 when Dad passed, how awesome is it that I had the experiences that I did with my parents? How awesome is it that for 28+ years they poured into me, such that the overflow could hold me in the years I'd have to live without them being physically present? What a glorious God we serve who traded my prayers of uncertainty with blessed assurance.

Even with God's blessed assurance, after Mom died, I remember "forgetting" how to pray for myself. I still spoke to God daily, finding something to thank Him for and filling any prayer requests that came my way, but as for praying for myself, it didn't happen. You see, I'd prayed for God to heal Mommy, but she still died. How do you form prayers to God when your reality reflects a situation in which you don't feel your prayers are being answered? How do you pray for joy from the One you naively think is responsible for taking your joy away? How exactly do you pray? For what exactly was I supposed to pray? I knew God and loved Him, but I didn't feel too high on His priority list.

These debilitating thoughts and painful talks with God treaded my lips until a warm morning in November when Dad was given a fatal diagnosis at

UNC Hospital. As the words "complete Kidney Failure" rolled off the doctor's lips, warm tears rolled down my face just as they had in that hospital room three months prior. "I am so sorry, Ms. Ward" the doctor started, "I know you've been through a lot here lately"

Much of that day is a blur, but I vividly recall calling out the name of "Jesus." No matter how deep my sorrow, one thing I knew for sure was that there was power in the name of Jesus and that I was still covered by His blood; I knew if I could just call on His name, it would suffice until I could articulate a prayer; until I could find the strength and the words to give meaning to the way that I felt.

Looking back, I can say that calling on the name of "Jesus" was *enough*. In the weeks that followed Dad's diagnosis, God taught me how to pray again. No, they weren't the formal, fancy prayers, but they were the prayers of my heart; I learned that every conversation I'd had with God since Mom died, counted; That whether I was calling on the name "Jesus" or simply sitting in His presence, it counted. I started praying the Psalms (the lament and Imprecatory Psalms were my favorite); I read the "Jesus Calling" devotional by Sarah Young that Mom had purchased for me months prior; I started listening to online sermons each morning; I chose a book of the Bible to study daily and refused to let the text go, until it meant something to me.

During this time, God gave language to my *muted prayers* and reconciled my grief and lack of understanding regarding Mom's passing and Dad's illness. God showed me that my prayers for Mom's deliverance was answered, it just wasn't in the way I expected; for death is the fulfillment of a promise from God. Perhaps it was in Mom's death that I forgot how to pray, but it was in Dad's sickness (leading up to his death) that I received the ultimate reminder.

I was sitting on the front row of my Systematic Theology class at Candler School of Theology at Emory University when I got the call that Dad had taken ill. You must understand that the Sunday prior, Dad had come with me to a preaching engagement in Apex, NC. His steps were slow, his breathing stressed. "Dad, we need to go to the doctor," I pleaded. Shaking his head, "Naw, I'm alright."

Perhaps it was the tears that glossed over my eyes; maybe it was the slight tremor in my hands as I gathered my belongings or even the look of defeat on my face, but somehow somebody in the class knew that the call I received wasn't a good one; someone in the class knew I needed prayer. Between sliding a note to the Teaching Assistant expressing that I had an emergency and running down the stairs of the building, my heart raced with a million questions that made me feel as if I couldn't get to North Carolina quick enough. Rushing from the campus parking lot with my GPS set on Hartfield Jackson Airport, I got a text from a classmate that left me speechless. Apparently, after leaving class my professor, Dr. Noel Erskine, stopped the class and prayed. Literally, every student in that 25-person class stood in a circle; stood in agreement for the healing of my father and my safe travel. I'd love to say this happens at every seminary or around any group of people, but I know that's not the case. My location at the time I received the daunting call was completely orchestrated by God. You see, I could have been anywhere, in any class and around any group of people. Yet, God placed me in a room of intercessors who knew how to call on the name "Jesus."

I still receive calls, text messages, emails and cards from people expressing their prayers of hope and comfort. While I will never be able to fully articulate the depth of my gratitude to my peers and professors at Candler School of Theology, I live daily with the knowledge and assurance that their continued prayers have contributed greatly to my livelihood and healing; their prayers have always and will always make a *difference* in my life.

CHAPTER 7:

How I met my Father

Through my mid-20s it would have been an overstatement to say I was "close" to my dad. I lived and breathed my mom; she was my entire world and though I loved my dad, I made little room for him in my world. You see, Dad had a hot temper and hazel eyes that could cut. He could be sweet as pie or as mean as a bull, but despite his mood on any given day, he was a man full of love.

Dad said "I love you" daily, but he showed love differently than Mom. He wasn't the "warm" or "empathetic" father. Instead, he was the father who said what was on his mind, while staring a hole right through you. If he was mad, you knew it. If he was happy, you knew it. He was predictable and I knew his moods without ever knowing how much he loved our family; I knew his moods without ever knowing him.

I often joke around and say that the four months between Mom's and Dad's death was the time that I "met" my father. For the first time in 28 years, I "met" a Dad who I enjoyed being around, laughing with and confiding in. For the first time, I met a Dad who I leaned on for emotional support; I met a supportive Dad who wanted to know about my day and didn't miss a single preaching engagement; I met a Dad who despite it all, made me feel like everything was going to be OK. Prior to Dad, Mom was the only one in the world who ever provided such assurance and comfort for me. Yet, the comfort with Dad was mutual.

From August 2016 to November 2016, I traveled home to North Carolina from Atlanta three to four days a week. Thankfully, Dad and Mom had some sort of agreement that if anything ever happened to her, Dad would move to one of those independent living locations. At least, that's what Dad told me. Having Dad at a supervised residence was a relief that came with uncertainty. It wasn't a nursing home, but it felt like it in some ways. No, there weren't nurses and the residents were active retirees, but there was a part of me wondered if I was making the right decision. I wondered if Dad was lonely when I wasn't around; I wondered if perhaps I should move back home and purchase a house that he could move into with me; I wondered if I was being selfish trying to stay in school. These thoughts tormented me, all the while in my heart of hearts I knew I was absolutely doing the right thing.

Every Friday when I'd arrive to Dad's residence, he would be waiting for me. You see, Dad would call ahead wanting to know the exact time I would be in town and you better believe that when I pulled up, he was ready with a ball cap, jeans and his khaki-colored Members Only Jacket. Sometimes he would even have his friends or some of the employees come to my car to say "Hello." It never failed that their "Hello" was followed by a "congratulations" of whatever accolade I'd told Dad about for the week. Dad never could keep good news to himself. Week after week, as Dad got in my car, he would always start complaining about how low my coupe sat to the ground as he arranged his six-foot stature into my bucket seats. Yet, through all the complaining he would stop, stare at me and then say, "Hey baby" or "You are so beautiful" or "You make me think of my momma."

Our outings were never too complex as they only consisted of Target, church or an occasional meeting regarding the estate. Dad never cared where we went, he just valued our time together. There were countless times we would be in the car together saying nothing at all. He'd be looking out of the window in deep thought and I would ask, "Daddy, what are you thinking about?" to which he would respond "Just talkin' to God." Moments later he would turn to me and say, "You look like you are thinking, Baby." A relationship that at one time had been so tense and complex was made simple and functioned with ease.

When November hit, Dad was given the fatal diagnosis of Kidney Failure with only four weeks to live. Sure, I knew he had Diabetes, which he refused to control. For years this, too, was rooted in my dismay for him as I'd watch him sneak doughnuts, cookies and sodas into his bedroom. A time or two when I'd gotten the courage to "stand up" to him, I'd say "Daddy, that food is going to kill you!" He'd frown, roll his eyes and keep doing whatever he was doing. It frustrated me that he never wanted help; it angered me that he didn't take care of himself better, which to me resulted in Mom going out of her way to take care of him. Now that I am married, I know it is not that easy. But from my "tween-age" years, it was my perspective.

That night in the hospital Dad declined Dialysis, which hit me like a sucker punch. No, I should not have been surprised, but it cut me like a dagger. I'd shifted my entire life to care for him in recent months, yet he wasn't willing to do Dialysis, the one thing I needed him to commit to, to take care of himself. Once again, I had a parent who was making their own parameters and decisions on how they would die with what felt like no consideration for me. Still in a fragile state from the loss of Mom months earlier, I was exhausted with my parents making these decisions on death, leaving me with the task of figuring out life without them. It all felt so premature and unfair.

With the sudden decline of Dad's health in early November, I moved back to North Carolina and made it my entire duty to care for and love on my Dad. Whether it was running errands for him, praying with him or simply rubbing his back as he threw up his own bile, I was committed to being there with him. He would often say, "Baby, you do so much for me" to which I would respond " It's because I love you, 'Daddy'! There's no one I'd rather do this for." He'd smile for we both knew that even in desperate times, love would conquer all.

Many days I sat in his room trying to make sense of it all. How was I to reconcile or make peace with the thought of losing my Dad? After living 28 years with a Dad I did not fully appreciate, I'd finally "met" the father I longed for; I met a father who I could joke with; I met a father who was patient and who I wanted around. I needed him so much, how could he leave me now?

Close family, friends and co-workers visited Dad in his last four weeks of life. Countless stories were told of fond memories that made us smile. I will never forget one of Dad's co-workers who, through tears of seeing Dad's frailty, said, "Kiya, one thing your Dad loved was his wife and kids." As Dad tuned in with an occasional nod and solemn smile, his co-worker told story after story about sacrifices Dad made throughout his life for our family. That's when it all started to come together for me; that's when I gained the understanding that the Dad I'd fallen head over heels for in four months had been there my entire life; this wasn't a "new" Dad, there was simply a new lens through which I was seeing him.

Amidst the laughter and smiles in the final visits, I will never forget the words of the Hospice nurse saying to me, "Kiya, I know your father is having a good week, but this is the calm before the storm." I suppose she'd seen it too many times before because within a day or two of her comment, Dad's health took an incredibly tragic turn. His organs began failing, his limbs stopped working and Dad lost control of his body. I saw the fear and frustration in those weak hazel eyes; the eyes that at one time could pierce through one's soul, now appeared desperate and frail.

In his final two weeks, I hired 24-hour caretakers to assist the in-home Hospice nurses with Dad's care. It would be multiple times throughout the night that I'd received calls, "Your father is in so much pain" or "His legs aren't working, but he keeps trying to get up and I'm scared he is going to fall" or "he has on no clothes." Dad was septic, which the nurse explained to me meant that without the ability to release toxins or fight infection, Dad's body was literally poisoning itself physically and mentally. His death would not happen all at once, but it would be long, slow and painful.

In Dad's final days he was transferred to a local Hospice facility. Dad stopped eating and the in-home Hospice Nurse and caretakers could no longer manage his pain. "How long can he go without food and water," I asked. With a new found allergy to Oxycodone that made Dad itch incessantly and Morphine that seemed to only partly dull the discomfort, the storm I was warned about was happening. Only, it was more like a tsunami overtaking him and destroying me.

The Hospice facility was meticulously clean, the staff was kind and there were bagged lunches and treats that local churches dropped off for families of Hospice patients. Not only did this place make patients comfortable, Hospice did everything they could to meet the immediate needs of the families. In the next few days, I'd go through the motions, preparing myself for the inevitable.

By this time, Dad was doing a lot of sleeping, yet there are two wakeful occurrences that are so vivid for me. The first occurred when he awoke asking me to come by his bed, "Momma, I got to get ready," he said. "Daddy," I began, "You are already dressed. You have on your clean clothes, the nurses have already bathed and dressed you for the day." Releasing a sigh, he glanced down at his t-shirt, seemingly skeptical at his "readiness" for whatever he was preparing for that day. Soon, he drifted back off to sleep.

The next day, I would be reading an article for class when out of nowhere Dad woke out of his sleep yelling, "Help! HONEY HELP!" Jumping up from the oversized brown leather recliner, I found myself at his bedside, startled, yet determined to keep my cool. "Daddy, what's wrong," I asked as calmly as I could muster. Yelling as loudly and aggressively as he could he said "HELP! I NEED HELP! HONEY HELP!" With terror and anguish, his hazel eyes locked with my deep brown gaze as he'd continue yelling, "HELP!"

At his demand for what I could not give, my eyes couldn't help but fill with tears, though I couldn't let the dew fall from my eyes. For after months of doing all I could for Dad, I was in a place where I could no longer provide the help he needed. All I could do was promise everything would be "OK" as I took a seat beside his bed and started praying and interceding for peace. Dad soon drifted off into a sleep from which he would not awake.

There are many hypotheses that would give reason to my father's final plea for "HELP," but I believe Dad was running from death that day. Yes, he was a Christian and already knew he was dying, but I believe that in seeing the angel of death appear, perhaps his time seemed a bit under-calculated; perhaps though ready in the flesh, his heart longed to do just a little bit more while here on earth.

One of the final words I heard Dad say was "Help" and the irony of it all is that "help" was the one thing I longed for; I wanted nothing more than to feel a type of "help" that would ease my pain and halt the horror of my reality, for it was "help" that I'd been crying out for since Mom died.

On many occasions, since the loss of my parents, I've cried out for "Help" from God. You know, on those days when my prayers are muffled between a rush of tears and a lack of understanding; those days when I wake up under paralyzing emotions that feel simultaneously full and empty. The truth is that my desire for "help" continues to be the constant in my ongoing conversations with God. There is something about "help" that only God can provide; about a type of "help" that serves as a balm to my broken heart. While I can't describe it, I can feel it and anyone around me can see it. God's help is what allows me to get up each morning; God's help is what allows me to smile and find joy even in this season of my life; God's help wipes my tears and holds me close; God's help aligns me with the people needed to move forward in life; God's help is what allows me to still testify of God's goodness and grace even during traumatic loss.

I've spent countless days trying to understand every aspect of the loss of my parents'. Why did Mom go first? Why did Dad pass when he did? Though I have many unanswered questions, I know one thing for sure and that is that Mom died first as a sign of God's amazing grace. You see, if Dad had passed first I would have never had the opportunity to apologize to him for the years of not understanding or fully appreciating him; I would have never had the opportunity to be with him and care for him; I would have never had the opportunity to "meet" my father.

The week after Dad passed was like a crashing train-I called out of all family gatherings, cancelled my counseling sessions, silenced my phone and tried to shut off mentally and emotionally. Though the funerals were over, my hyper-active thoughts were just beginning. For weeks, I juggled feelings of loneliness, resentment, despair and failure. After Dad died, I'd looked forward to getting through the funeral so that I could just "think," but instead I found my own thoughts suffocating. I remember getting up the morning after Dad's funeral and as I walked to the kitchen window, I asked my best friend, "What am I supposed to do now" to which she responded "Nothing." It was then that I realized that the road to healing wasn't about me taking control of my life, it was about submitting all control to God. I knew I had to submit my feelings to God, but how? I didn't *feel* like being around people or even talking on the phone; I didn't *feel* like reading the Bible; and I only went on social media to mentally escape from my own reality.

After a week of doing "nothing" my bestie and I decided to head to Miami for the holidays. I knew that my favorite holiday was coming and the last thing I wanted was to be home for Christmas. Christmas for our family was more than just a few minutes of exchanging gifts. Christmas for our family included multiple nights of social gatherings (Mom loved entertaining); it was opening gifts on Dec 24th, so that we could spend Christmas Day celebrating Jesus without distraction; it was going to Lifeway to get the perfect Christmas cards to send out; it was last minute shopping and a special dinner on the 26th in remembrance of my maternal grandfather's birthday. Having all of these rituals come to a sudden halt was something I just wasn't ready to embrace. As a result, I did what at that time felt best, I escaped.

My time in Miami was well spent. I ate overpriced food, laid under a massive umbrella on the beach and for the first time since I can remember, I kept my phone off an entire night. In my young adult life, Mom always told me to keep my phone on throughout the night in case of an emergency. So, I did. I kept it on to receive the call that Dad was taking worse. I kept it on to receive the call that Dad died. I even kept it on as family came into town around the funeral. Yet, after the funeral, I came to the quick realization that I was the one facing the emergency and I was in dire need of silence. I needed to "turn off" my phone and when, for the first time, I did, I took a deep breath. I exhaled expectations of others and breathed in the still air of uncertainty. Turning off my phone all night meant that no emergency calls were expected; no one was fully relying on me; and for the first-time in a long time, I was my main priority.

On Christmas night, I sat on the furnished rooftop terrace of my Miami hotel overlooking the beautiful downtown lights. As I sat and prayed, I began to cry. "God, why?" I pleaded, "Why would you let this happen?" As warm tears streamed down my sun-kissed skin, words began to pour off my lips. Words of anger, frustration and resentment flowed like a river as I poured my anguish at God's feet. I was angry with God and had been since Mom died, yet I had been too proud to tell God; I was too worried about being "wrong" or "sinful" but I had a bone to pick with God and it wasn't until I was hundreds of feet in the air that I found the courage to throw the first punch; the courage to submit my feelings to God.

On that rooftop, I learned that submitting my feelings to God was about humbling myself and exposing my hurt to Him; it was saying "GOD HELP!" and allowing Him to come into my heart to heal me. God wasn't looking for my "perfectly polished" prayer, He was looking for my honesty, vulnerability and genuine desire for Him; He was looking for my "ugly cry face" ; the deep groan that came when I no longer had words to express my pain; and the focus of my eyes when I had nowhere else to look but toward a dark sky lit up by Miami lights. God wanted me and everything that I encompassed.

When I came down from the rooftop terrace, I went to sleep with the residue of damp tears lingering on my face. Yet, I woke up with a spurt of energy that certainly caught me by surprise. While still in bed, I grabbed my calendar and started writing out plans God had for my life. This girl who hours prior couldn't even think of the next day was suddenly enamored with the months to come. I can't say I woke up filled with joy, but I was filled with the next best thing-EXPECTATION! God had a plan for me; God had a future for me. Psalm 30:5 reads, "Weeping may endure for a night, but joy comes in the morning." For the first time in months I felt like my *morning* was coming! I began to "smell" it; embrace it; and receive it.

When I lost my parents, I thought I'd lost my life, my future, and my promise. But I now see that losing my parents only shifted me to better align me with God's plan for my life. I am still on course, my destiny remains un-touched, and though not here in the flesh, my parents will always be with me on this journey called life.

CHAPTER 8:

Celebrations

Christmas and birthdays are my favorite times of the year. As a young adult, I literally planned for months to execute a three to four-week celebration of life, culminating with friends and family gathered on my actual birthday (Oct. 22). My birthday gives me a reason to fellowship with friends and family that I don't get to see on a regular basis. However, as you can imagine, my 2016 birthday was a bit different.

The weeks prior to my birthday were spent taking care of family business, while balancing school, family and jobs. The days prior were spent mostly in tears as I dreaded this "first" birthday without my mother. I missed her calls asking "So what did you and your friends do to celebrate today"; I missed hearing Mom laughing at how serious I took my celebration; I missed Mommy calling to clarify when I'd be coming home; I missed Mommy more than ever.

I remember telling Dad, "You know next week is my birthday," to which he smiled and nodded his head. It was his solemn reply that reminded me that this birthday would be different. For once, this type-A planner didn't plan a thing. I didn't plan extravagant dinners, I didn't have all my friends fly in, I didn't rent or reserve anything. Everything was very last minute and more so "I'm hungry, we should probably get food tonight" (I thank God for friends who didn't need much of a heads up).

The face of my phone shattered the night before my birthday, but I still woke up to back-to-back dings notifying me of birthday wishes on my phone. Unfortunately, instead of garnering the usual excitement, the noise made me incredibly anxious. You see, the last time I'd received back-to-back dings on my phone was the morning after Mom died. And just like that, I [mentally] went from being in my Atlanta apartment back to the hospital room with Mom's lifeless body. Needless to say, my shattered phone immediately went on silent for the rest of the day. To this day, three years later, back to back dings on my phone serves as an emotional trigger for me. As a result, I keep group chats muted, limit phone notifications from Apps and often keep my phone on silent.

Even after fixing my phone, I answered very few calls on my birthday. In all honesty, I wasn't ready to hear the "I know this one is going to be hard" or the awkward silence after "I know this is the first without..." I felt the gap and there was something about the thought of hearing loved ones on the other end of that dial that made me incredibly sad. Perhaps it was that their vocal presence maximized Mom's silence; perhaps talking on the phone that day made things too real. No matter how many calls or text I received, I knew the most important one would be missing; for the first time in forever, "Mommy" would not pop-up on my phone, there would be no special flower or Edible Arrangement delivery; there would be no "cake in a jar"...the only "gift" from Mom on my first birthday without her was life itself... but perhaps the gift of life was the greatest gift of all.

Even now, before any holiday I am faced with the decision of exactly how to spend the occasion. Do I go out of town? Do I keep my normal routine? What about Mother's Day? As a child, my mother would take my siblings and I to our grandmother's house before church on Mother's Day. We would go not to stay, but to cut roses from her rose bushes. The red roses were for my siblings and I, but my grandmother would cut a white rose. Mom explained the purpose behind this tradition and it honestly didn't mean much to me until this Mother's Day when I was given a white rose.

The year following Mom's death, I returned to a church in Hillsborough, NC where Mom and I preached together a few Mother's Days ago - Mommy preached the first 15 minutes and then I closed. On this particular Mother's Day, as I sat in the pulpit without Mom, I noticed the empty space where Mom would have sat. I glanced at the Deacon's corner where Dad used to be. As the choir stood to give the pre-sermonic song, I noticed something even more familiar than the empty seats. The pianist started playing the song "Going Up Yonder." Mind you, that's the same song that was sung as my mother's body was pushed from the altar to the cemetery at her Homegoing Service. Everything within me wanted to crumble; I wanted to lose it; I wanted to ball up in the fetal position. Yet, none of that happened. My worst fears did not manifest. Instead, I wiped my tears and took the song as a beautiful reminder of my parents' presence with me on that first Mother's Day without them.

It goes without saying that celebrations without my parents are "weird." Thus, graduation was no different. If anything, it was one of the harder milestones to celebrate. You see, unlike other celebrations I've experienced since their deaths, seminary was something that my parents started off with me. They were both so proud of me for attending Emory and pursuing full time ministry. I recall so vividly after learning of Mom's fatal diagnosis, I told her "Mom, I am taking off a semester to take care of you!" Mom wasn't having it.

"Kiya," she exclaimed, "I won't be here." I thought she meant "here" as in the state of sickness; I thought she was professing her faith that she would be healed and would not need me to care for her. Hours later I learned that "here" was in reference to being physically present on earth.

Yet, in the weeks leading up to my graduation I found myself "here" and wanting nothing more than my parents to be "here" with me. I didn't send out any invitations nor did I plan a huge celebration. My amazing husband was so excited for me and my closest friends made their way to Atlanta without my nudging. It was like everyone just kind of fell into place without my orchestration. Even my graduation photos were taken very last minute, as we happened to have a photo shoot planned for something else and George brought my cap and gown. After graduation, I literally went back to our Airbnb and slept. There was no festive dinner or Atlanta shopping. I was so grateful for the degree, but going through the motions of graduation exhausted all of my energy and took everything I had. I wasn't sad; I wasn't upset. I just wanted to sleep.

Within a month of graduation, it was Dad's birthday. Dad hated celebrating his birthday, yet for some reason not even having the option of celebrating it with him was agonizing. I thought back on two years prior when I'd called Dad to wish him a happy birthday from the Bahamas. Knowing that Dad always went to sleep early, I called a bit earlier than to make sure he was awake. "Hey Baby, Baby!" he answered as Mom passed him the phone. "Hey Daddy- Happy Birthday! I hate that I can't be there to celebrate with you." With a grin I could hear through the phone he replied, "Ohh I know what you doin'. You are over there preachin', teachin', talkin' to God, and helpin' people and that makes me feel soooooo good." I chuckled with an affirmative, "Yes Daddy, that's exactly what I'm doin'."

I still smile as I think of that interaction with Dad. Though I don't write about him as often as Mom, Dad was a huge supporter of me in ministry. He was literally at every preaching engagement that was within driving distance (He'd tag along with Mom) and on those engagements that were too far or too late or too whatever for him to attend, I'd always get a call or word of encouragement, "Kiya, did the people like your preachin'? I know they did!" On November 6, Dad was feeling ill, yet was determined to attend my preaching engagement. I spoke with him the evening before, "Dad, I know you don't feel good. I'll be alright" To which he responded, "What time you gonna pick me up?" Little did I know that November 6th, 2016 would be the last sermon Dad heard prior to his death and the last time I'd have a parent in the audience to hear me preach.

CHAPTER 9:

Lost

I was one of those people who had a specific 10-year plan for my life- three degrees by 30, "MRS." by 31, kids by 36, four degrees by 40...you get the picture. The canvas of my life was complete and all I needed was a bit of patience and faith...or so I thought. Yet, the death of my parents made me question every plan and purpose in my life. Things I'd previously enjoyed, I enjoyed no longer; hobbies became arduous to complete; and even taking time to focus my attention on something took more effort than I knew how to exert.

Prior to the passing of Mom and Dad, I never had trouble paying attention to anything. In all honesty, I probably paid too much attention to details in life. Keeping this in mind, you can understand why I found my sudden lack of focus exhausting. Something as normal to me as reading a book became an overwhelming feat juggling the words of the book with my wandering thoughts. It was like I could be sitting in a room and my thoughts would somehow take my senses back to my last view of Mom or to the face of Dad. Each time, these adventurous thoughts resulted in unfinished reads and tears flowing from my eyes. Even trying to complete a paper for class seemed impossible as I'd gone from being a writing tutor for my seminary to having constant writer's block. I felt like I was mentally and emotionally paralyzed with the daunting feeling that these feelings would never end. Needless to say, in a world where I thought I'd found my purpose, I felt completely *lost*.

Unexpected trauma and disappointment have a way of making one question every bit of "normalcy" in life. Things that were once so "sure" quickly become areas of uncertainty, which cultivates a feeling of one being *lost*. Going into seminary, I had my life plan figured out (don't all 26-year-olds!). I just knew that after completing seminary I would get a pastoral placement and eventually work as a staff pastor at my church in North Carolina. I completed internships, maintained competitive grades and took advantage of professional development opportunities, all geared toward this path that I knew I was destined to take, only it wasn't destiny. One of the first things that changed when my parents died was the trajectory of my career. My call to senior pastorate fell silent and my energy toward that goal was depleted. Now, not only was I lost without my parents, but I did not even have a clear career path. I truly was lost. Feeling *lost* was terrifying for it was unlike anything I'd ever felt. I wasn't used to walking so long in the dark. Yet, I've come to learn that in dark places, God's light still shines and shows me the way.

I can't say exactly when the "light turned on" for my revised career path, but it was somewhere between writing my blog and getting hired at my dream job the year after their passing. Mom used to always tell me, "Kiya, the day you stop dreaming is the day you die." Serving as a Staff Pastor at Mount Zion Baptist Church of Greensboro was my dream job...only I didn't envision myself working in this capacity until I was 40 or 50. What do you do when the dream job you hope to get in your 40s is given to you at 29? I asked my then fiancé this very question, to which he responded "you keep dreaming." Dreaming was hard for me because to dream meant that I had to think about my future and to think about my future meant that I had to do it without Mom and Dad being physically present. Dreaming of my future felt like a series of "Plan B" efforts, with all of my "Plan A" thrown out with my parents' death.

My spiritual father, Bishop Bryan J. Pierce, Sr., once preached a sermon in which he said "Your plan B was God's plan A the entire time." Wow! As those words pierced my heart, I realized that I didn't have to have everything "figured out." The truth is, it was ok for me to dream, to think on my future, without knowing every single in and out; without seeing all of the resources needed and without knowing exactly how the vision would come together. It was ok for me to dread exciting parts of my future knowing my parents would not be present with me physically. However, dreading their lack of presence was not the same as dreading an actual endeavor. For example, I could still be excited about one day getting married, even though I knew Dad would not walk me down the aisle; and I could still one day be a best-selling author, even without Mom to proof read the pages of my book. At this revelation, I found a new layer in the *grace to grieve* as I gave myself the grace to dream; the grace to think about my future. In embracing this grace, I learned that timelines are comforting, but God's timeline is perfect. Actually, I've found it better not to have life figured out as it requires me to submit my life daily to God; it requires me to allow God to reveal the canvas of my life in His own timing. Sure, I am eager to see what the future holds and I'd love to know its intricacies, but there is a peace in knowing who holds my future; there is a peace in knowing that I am no longer *lost*.

CHAPTER 10:

Courage

I recently learned of a colleague in ministry who unexpectedly lost a member of their immediate family. When I heard the news, my eyes locked with my iPhone, my heart sunk and I was at a loss for words. I didn't know their deceased spouse, but I knew that immediate feeling of shock. Every time I hear of someone dying, I am reminded of the initial shock and disbelief. While I can relate with the feelings of loss, I never really know what to say to the person experiencing grief. I get dozens of emails asking for advice "Pastor Kiya, how do I get through this loss?" and "Pastor Kiya, what do I do now in the wake of my loved one dying?" Ironically, even though I have what I consider to be an almost "too close" connection to death, I feel far from the expert. Even in Pastoral care sessions as people lament over their loved one, I find myself nodding and simply taking in their words and emotions. The truth is, in the grace to grieve there is courage; courage to share feelings and articulate the rush of emotions at hand. Thus, the person who emails or even schedules a time to meet with me has already shown more courage than I could ever teach them. You see, in the grieving process, there is a manifestation of strength. However, strength isn't in holding in emotions or knowing what to say, it is in embracing every moment that you don't know what to say; strength is articulating emotions in the best way you can, even when the explanation isn't audible.

I recall leaving the gravesite after Mom's funeral and locking eyes with one of my best friends, "Jigga." In that moment, Jigga already knew I'd given all I had to attend the viewing and make it through the funeral. As far as I could see, I didn't have anything left. As I fell into her arms and she held me tight, she kept repeating the words Mom said to me hours before her passing, "You are stronger than you think." "Kiya," Jigga repeated with tears running down her own face, "Mom was right. You are so much stronger than you think." It was in that moment when I didn't feel as if I had strength left that God blessed me with a support system who spoke strength into my life. The truth is, to this day my proximity still speaks strength into my life; my proximity still speaks life to me on the days when I feel lifeless. It is this truth that has given me courage in my grief, while sparking me to speak courage to others. One thing that is for sure in this life is that everyone is going through "something."

I understand that losing both parents is tragic, but along this journey I've gained so much strength and courage from people going through things I could not imagine. Just think about the teen who is facing HIV, the woman in the beauty shop who lost her father and husband within two months, the newlyweds who miscarried their first born and the person newly diagnosed with an aggressive cancer. People are going through STUFF and making it every step of the way.

I find strength in the courageous men and women I encounter on a daily basis who are pushing through life's trials and tribulations. No two seasons of life are comparable, so I dare not suggest one season to be better or worse than another. However, I can say that there is so much to learn from others who are going through their own seasons of life with grace, endurance and love. Never forget that the way you go through your season can be the very thing that gives strength and courage to someone pressing their way through their life.

CHAPTER 11:

Weight

D eath takes much more than an emotional toll on those left to grieve. The impact of my parents' death was just as much physical as it was emotional. In the four months between Mom and Dad's death, I gained 20 pounds (an additional five pounds after Dad died). It's not that I sat up eating all night, but being on the road three to four days a week left me few options outside of fast food and the comfort treats found in the airport. Not to mention, there is something about a milk chocolate candy bar with caramel that I found very hard to resist! Sure, there were healthy options at restaurants, but fried foods just tasted better. Soon, my clothes were fitting tighter, then not at all. Shopping was not an option as I refused to go up a dress size in the store (I can be stubborn).

Aside from the physical weight, I started noticing random hairs on my face. These hairs turned into patches of hair, which apparently is a common result of unmanaged stress (I thank God for laser hair removal *smiles*). Quickly, I found myself not only in a world that didn't seem like my own, but I was trapped in a body that was not familiar to me.

For anyone who has struggled with weight-loss, you know that it's not an overnight process. It's a constant up and down of judging your worth by the numbers on the scale. It's the juxtaposition of wanting to purchase new clothes that have a better fit, but being too prideful to go up a dress size; it is the juxtaposition of wanting to work out, but desiring to savor a fresh blowout (can I get an Amen!). Right before my eyes I'd become someone I didn't quite recognize in the mirror. I needed help.

I hired three personal trainers within one year, none who could keep off the weight that emotional eating was feeding incessantly between weight training and cardio. It soon hit me that to lose the physical weight, I had to lose my stubbornness and pride; I had to change my mindset as well as my relationship with eating. Junk food had become my Achilles heel and I was killing myself with food. I knew high blood pressure and diabetes ran in my family, yet I couldn't seem to stop the high sodium foods or cupcakes.

At my peak, I gained a total of 50 pounds within the year following Mom's and Dad's death. The weight gain was embarrassing, frustrating and seemingly impossible to lose. I felt guilty for gaining the weight and defeated at what appeared to be my inability to lose the weight.

I'd love to say that I have lost the weight; that all 50 pounds are completely gone. But that would be a lie. The reality is, I didn't gain 50 pounds in one day and I can't lose it in one day. Sure, I've lost some of the weight, but I still have a way to go to get where I need to be with my weight. However, I am encouraged that while I am not where I want to be, I am also not where I used to be. I am in a more disciplined space that is free of guilt and where I strive to be the healthiest version of myself. I monitor my blood pressure, make yearly doctor's visits and meal prep (that's a whole other book!). Long story short, I am giving myself not only the grace to grieve, but the grace to be human.

CHAPTER 12:

Learning to "Be"

My mother was like a trough in which I placed the burdens of my life. Mom had a way of seeing through my "I'm fine" and getting to the core of whatever frivolous worry I'd allowed to take over my mind. When at the root, Mom would pray for me and speak to whatever the circumstance. It never failed that no matter how "big" the situation, hearing Mom say, "Kiya, everything is going to be alright" felt like soothing ointment to my soul. If she said it, I believed it.

Among her soothing quotes was one she would often say in times of trouble, "Kiya, it's not a death." She compared every situation to death to expose the truth that no matter what I was facing, there was someone facing much worse; that no matter what I was facing, there was someone saying a *final* goodbye. Comparing everyday trials and tribulations to someone facing the death of a loved one has a way of shrinking everyday worries to minimal concerns. Just think, "He doesn't like me" compared to "I need to write my mother's obituary"; "I can't believe he/she did that" compared to "I will never feel the embrace of my parent again" or "I don't know how my bills are going to be paid" compared to "I watched my parents' casket go into the ground." For me, death was always the "worst" case scenario that made any situation I was facing seem "not so bad"...only this time it was *death* and it was *bad*.

The death of my parents aroused a pain that I didn't know existed. It stung, it cut, it bruised, it lingered, it burned, it suffocated and it hurt...all at the same time. There were times I cried inconsolably and times that I couldn't cry at all; times when I felt the weight of the world on my back and times when I was numb from all the pain. The ups and downs of polarizing emotions was exhausting and all I could say was "It *is* a death."

With the whirlwind of emotions, I knew I needed more than the "ear" of devoted friends, but I didn't have the courage to go to counseling right away. You see, prior to Mom's death I had a very hypocritical relationship with the idea of counseling. Truthfully, I'd encourage others to receive counseling, but I felt "ashamed" going on my own. Counseling was something for people who needed "help" and as a minister surely God was all the help I needed, right?

I will never forget the first time I called to make a counseling appointment. The Administrative Assistant answered the phone and through tears, a shaky voice and a huge gulp in my throat I said, "My name is Kiya Ward and I just lost my mom and I need help making sense of everything." I was at my most vulnerable point and honestly that was about as much as I could get out without completely losing it over the phone. Within the same week, I met the woman who would be my therapist. She was a beautiful African American woman with chocolate skin and almond-colored eyes. She had a smile that could light up a room and warmth that only a mother could exude. She had a tone in her voice that commanded one's attention and an elegance that reminded me so much of my mom. To this day I count my therapist among my greatest gifts from God as she normalized counseling by helping me understand that although God was the root of my help, He also used vessels (i.e.: licensed professionals) to strengthen and encourage me on my restorative journey toward healing. Most importantly, my therapist taught me how to "be."

Learning how to "be" has been one of the most challenging (yet fundamental) parts of my healing process. You see, I am my mother's daughter (and my grandmother's granddaughter), which means that I've been bred with the highest level of lady-like decorum. Unfortunately, this type of decorum doesn't lend space for one to "be." The lady-like decorum that I embraced focused more on the "appearance" of emotions than the "reality" of them; it meant keeping in feelings that could be perceived as *weak* and always remembering that a smile and appropriate attire conceals most emotions from the human eye. Shifting this ideology didn't come over night, but I soon learned what it meant to "be."

I learned that to "be" meant breaking the shackles of societal expectations of "lady-like" decorum surrounding my emotions. For me, it meant that if I didn't feel like being around people, I wasn't rude for saying "no"; that even if I had 18 missed calls, 13 voicemails and 43 text messages to which I did not respond, I was not impolite; I wasn't "weak" for crying, I wasn't "ungrateful" for being sad, and I wasn't "rude" for being anti-social. I was simply learning to "be."

Learning how to "be" is the way that I give myself permission to unapologetically grieve and to be human in the face of such great loss; learning how to "be" is the *nakedness* in my intimate relationship with God and my *reality* with the world; learning how to "be" was the catalysis in establishing my new normal; it was the way I overcame the "sorry" of so many people.

One of my greatest apprehensions over the last three years has been people feeling *sorry* for me. Petty, right? It should be the least of my worries, but the thought of people feeling "sorry" for me puts a lump right in the center of my throat (it's the "Audrey Lee" in me). It is the good-intentioned "sorry" that leaves an awkward silence during conversations when people didn't quite know how to gauge my smile or can't think of the quote, they meant to recite to me.

Death has a debilitating quality that makes those left behind feel "stuck." It's like trying to put together a jigsaw puzzle knowing that you are missing the integral pieces. With every "I'm so sorry" I am reminded of the challenge of putting the pieces back together; strangers asking detailed questions of my everyday life to satisfy their "sorry" is invasive; it's torture. "I'm sorry" was appropriate at the funeral, but now (years later), it is a soundtrack that has no place in my daily playlist. Instead of speaking through one's "sorry", I prefer people speak into my future. For example, my makeup artist recently said, "Girl, I can't wait to see what God has in store for you"; and just the other day my best friend said, "So next year when you..." Every time people speak into my future I take in a breath of fresh air; every time people speak into my future, they speak into my *new normal*.

One of the re-occurring words of comfort offered to me during the death of my parents was "You will find your 'new normal.'" I wasn't quite sure what it meant and I wasn't sure I wanted to know. I didn't want a new normal, I wanted my old normal back. I wanted Mom to call me every day and I wanted to call Dad fussing about him sneaking doughnuts into the house (he was diabetic); I wanted to look into Dad's hazel eyes, feel mom's warm smile and linger in their embrace. I wanted my old normal, but had no choice but to embrace something new.

Moving forward has its pros. I am no longer planning funerals or making burial arrangements; I am no longer driving between Atlanta and North Carolina every weekend; I am no longer spending the entirety of my days in estate meetings. Instead, I sleep with my phone on silent, I'm reading books I had put to the side, I'm enjoying my life as a newlywed and I am progressing in ministry. Needless to say, my life is moving forward.

Moving forward is refreshing and liberating, but it is also scary. There is always a part of me that looks toward my parents for their input in everyday decisions. Mom and I used to sit and dream for hours, making a bucket list for some of our most exciting plans in life. Yet, as these plans come into fruition, I long to share them with her. When I met my incredible husband, I wanted nothing more than to bring him home to meet my parents. I wanted Mom to comment on his looks and spirituality; I wanted Dad to show him his guns (so embarrassing lol). When I passed Catechism, I wanted to call Mom screaming with excitement; Whenever I travel, I still pick up my phone to call Mom to let her know I made it safely. I am moving forward in this "new normal" but it is still weird, awkward and uncomfortable.

On the average day, I don't think about the death of my parents. Instead, I think of them being alive and very much present in my day-to-day endeavors. I think of funny comments from Mom and hilarious facial expressions from Dad. I think of their advice and often consider what they would "say" when making decisions. I don't think on my parents with sadness, but it is the flashbacks that pull so tightly at my heart.

Although 90% of the flashbacks I have of my parents are positive, there are 10% that are daunting. The flashback of Mom's final moments; the flashback of me running down the hall to get the doctor; the flashback of Mom's lifeless body under the sheet being pushed into the morgue; the flashback of me screaming on the phone with my uncle in distress; closing Mom's casket at her funeral; Dad's sunken cheeks; Dad's cries for "help"; both of their caskets being lowered into the ground. Those are the scenes etched in my mind that I will never be able to forget...and I am not sure I want to.

You see, it is the flashbacks that are daunting, but the flashbacks also remind me of what God has brought me through. I literally had a seat at death's table and lived to tell about it. There are many who don't get up from that seat; many who lose their minds at that seat. Yet, in those moments when I found myself emotionally lifeless, God kept me, covered me and breathed life into me.

There are many who have flashbacks to their past and are left in a state of distress, regret and pain. Yet, there is a power that arises when you can think on your toughest and most tragic moments without the moments themselves having power over you.

CHAPTER 13:

Manifestation

My mother and I were dreamers of life, love and ministry. We'd sit for hours just dreaming about things to come and expressing excitement about every little detail of my future. One of our favorite dreams to share was what my future husband would be like. We'd laugh and giggle about how strong he'd have to be to deal with my "independence," the sense of humor he'd have to handle my sarcasm and the love for God he'd have to fully support me in ministry. We'd smile, chatting about the tears Dad would have in his eyes the day he had to walk me down that long aisle of the Bennett Chapel (I've always wanted to get married there). Amidst our conversations, Mom would always remind me how she and Dad had been praying for my future spouse since I was a little girl. She never promised to know who "he" was, but she was confident in a God who heard their prayers.

When God sent my now husband, I was in awe. Beyond his witty humor, beautiful heart and love for God, there was something "different" about him. As I've prayed for God to reveal that "difference" to me, I've come to the beautiful realization that he is the *manifestation* of my parents' prayers. My parents not only left me with cherished memories, but through their prayers they left me with the most incredible husband.

There is an indescribable feeling of manifested prayers of loved ones who've passed. You know, those things that you prayed for together that your loved one isn't physically present to experience with you. I experience this regularly, like when I got my dream job that Mom and I prayed about; when George and I bought our first home; when I received an honor for preaching from Candler; and the list goes on. For each memorable experience in my world, I get an intense craving to pick up the phone and call Mom. A few times without thinking, I've picked up my phone to call Mom in excitement only to be jolted back into a reality that reminds me that I no longer have that luxury. Every now and then, not often, when I have something to tell Mom and Dad, I just say it. With no one around and no "proof" they can hear me, I just do as I saw Mom do, I tell something to my deceased parents.

My beautiful grandmother (maternal) passed in 2014 at the age of 100. My mother was very close to her, so I was very observant in her grieving process. Although I never saw my mother cry, she would often say "Kiya, I was talking to Mother this morning." I didn't really know how to respond and the idea of Mom being in pain was so obscure to me, so I'd just say, "Oh ok."

It wasn't until Mom died that I understood the gravity of talking to a deceased parent. It's not something that I regularly find comfort in, but it is something that I find comfort in knowing that I *can* do. It sounds sooooo weird, but ask anyone who has experienced loss. It is something about telling that deceased love one that you graduated, got a good grade or even got a new job that at times brings an unexpected peace. At other times, it brings frustration when you want nothing more than to have your loved one physically present with you.

CHAPTER 15:

Show Up

Today, while sitting in a Homegoing Service, it hit me that I've been to three funerals in the past four days. It is the plight of a pastor, yet still a sobering thought to think that three times in four days I've seen the stream of painful tears run down the faces of the bereaved; three times I've seen families take the final look at their loved one as the casket slowly closed; three times I've heard preachers give words of comfort to fill in the gaps of uncertainty and grief. I was only on the program at one of the services, yet in four days I've attended three funerals.

Honestly, I'm not a fan of funerals, but I attend them for the simple fact that there is power in showing up. I learned this power at the funerals of my parents as dozens and dozens of people showed up in respect, love and solidarity. Of course, many of the people were dear friends and loved ones, but several faces were only vaguely familiar.

As I sat gazing at my mother's lifeless body, I recall a shadow that caught my attention. As I broke the gaze to satisfy my curiosity, my eyes were greeted by a group of friendly faces from my church located an hour away. This would have been expected, only the faces I saw were not totally familiar. Instead, they were people who I had no idea would even show up. Leaders of my church and community who I didn't even know knew my name; classmates I hadn't seen in 10+ years; friends from out of state. People near and far showed up.

The truth is, my parents' funerals are a blur. I cannot tell you what scripture was read and I do not remember the sermon titles, but I do remember who showed up. To this very day, I thank God for each and every person who showed up.

This morning I sat in church as the names were read of those who recently transitioned. As I sat listening to the chorus of names, my heart bled for the families left to experience what I call the "nightmare." I wish I could find another word more peaceful and angelic, but honestly the days lingering between a loved one's death and their actual funeral is like living through a nightmare from which you cannot wake up. Every breath feels like your last and every thought is encompassed with a lack of control.

I remember dreading every moment I was awake following Mom's death. There was this understanding that I had to survive, but this relentless ambiguity in how I would. Waking up was painful; living was painful. It seemed like everything I did was a heavy reminder of the burdensome grief that was suffocating me. As much as I dreaded her death, I dreaded her funeral a million times more. Endless cards, calls, texts and messages came in promising prayers of comfort and relief, but even those became liken to a chorus of numb melancholy.

It's hard to say the exact moment in which this nightmare ends, for there are days even now that the nightmare resurfaces; days when I just want to sleep instead of be awake; days when I burst into unexpected tears; days when the burden of losing my parents still feels unbearable; days when I can literally hear Mom taking her final breath; days when I am living in a nightmare. Yet, despite those days of emotional claustrophobia, I always wake up. And as time passes, the days do not linger as long; the tears are more quickly wiped away, and I am reminded that my reality is better than any dream.

One of the most frequent questions I get from people outside of my immediate circle is, "How do you get through loss?" My answer really varies from person to person, but a recent tragedy led me to put my response in writing. So here it is, an open letter to that person navigating the loss of a loved one:

To: The person experiencing loss
From: A person experiencing loss

You are alive. Despite the feeling of being numb, dead, disconnected and out of control, you are alive. Every moment you are breathing is a moment that you are surviving. This means that you are already one step further than you thought you'd be. God is your complete life-support, for you can't do this season on your own. Yes, you are out of control. Yes, it feels unfair. Yes, God is still good and faithful, but it is normal to wonder where He is at a time like now; it is normal to wonder how or why and to explore your unanswered questions.

The phone calls and messages you are getting will eventually die down. For now, it is ok not to respond. It is ok to find grave annoyance at what is meant to be the helpful "God has it under control" and "I am praying for you." People mean well and while the messages seem redundant and empty right now, you will eventually look back and realize that the chorus of prayers is what kept you. Meanwhile, it is ok not to not to feel ok. It is ok to lack an understanding of God's purpose in this experience. It's ok to feel overwhelmed by the tasks to be done. It is ok. For now, give yourself the grace to grieve. Though they feel endless, your tears will stop. And yes, you will smile and laugh again. And after the laughter you will cry again...really hard. But you will re-discover joy and peace. You will feel guilty the first time you actually feel "ok." You will feel awkward at the unexpected feeling of liberation that comes with death, especially if you were the primary caretaker of your loved one. There will come a time when the memories scrolling through your mind slow down; when memories of your loved one are met with an unexpected laugh or a soft smile; a time when you let go not of the person, but of this "feeling" that is so daunting.

Most importantly, though it may not seem like it in this experience, you will learn so many new and unexpected dimensions of God's love and provision for you. You've met the God who took away, perhaps unexpectedly. Now, prepare to meet the God of restoration. Prepare to embark on unmarked territory to find your <u>new normal</u>. For now, your normal may be filled with tears, hopelessness, insecurity, fear, regret, indifference or even ambiguity. Soon, those feelings will be replaced with God's peace, God's <u>blessed assurance</u> and the re-assurance that you are ok. You will relinquish regret. Everything really is going to be ok.

Yours in Christ,

Kiya

CHAPTER 15:

Feelings

I am learning that one of the important keys to healing is moving beyond *feelings*. Yes, one has to embrace the varied emotions of fear, anger, disappointment, hurt, loss, rejection, etc. but at some point, one has to stop waiting on *feelings* to function. Just think, there are days you don't *feel* like going to work, but you go; days you don't *feel* like adulting, but you do; days you don't *feel* like worshipping at church, but you still raise holy hands (*can I get an "Amen"*); days you don't *feel* like going to class, but you show up; days you *feel* like completely going OFF, but you hold your peace; days you *feel* like giving up, but you keep pressing forward. If we were to rely solely on our *feelings*, what would get accomplished?

You see, this life isn't 100% about what we feel. Much of the time, it's about using faith to press through feelings that are debilitating and/or destructive. For me, on those days when my feelings seem stronger than my faith, I am reminded that though I feel weak, in Christ I am strong; though my life has shifted to a "Plan B" I am still in God's "Plan A." You see, I realize that many of my daunting *feelings* come not just from the loss of my parents, but in the uncertainty of how it impacts my future. In this vein, I am learning to press beyond my *feelings* to replace what "I don't know about the future with what I do know about God" (Catie Caine). As I replace daunting *feelings* of ambiguity with unwavering confidence in God, I can't help but notice my focus shifting from uncontrollable *feelings* to undeniable faith.

When I think back over the past three years, there is an undeniable faith that is threaded through every experience. I remember texting my best friend, Rebecca, as I wrote Mom's obituary. The text read something like, "Sis, I can't do this." At that moment, my faith was bewildered and I just knew my life was over. The idea of even thinking past the moment was exhausting. Yet, here I am three years later full of joy and peace.

It's been three years since I last saw the faces of my parents; three years since we prayed together; since they held my hand, made a joke and smiled so gently. There was a time, three years ago, that I was sure my world was completely over. Yet here I am, three years later, still as sure as ever of God's sovereignty and amazing grace; sure of God's restorative power. People have always asked how I can be so sure of God; and why I am so happy. I used to just smile and revert the conversation in a desire not to get "too deep." But in recent months, I've found the answer, which I can now clearly articulate. You see, now that I know what it's like to lose my joy, I can confidently proclaim that joy is a gift from God. The fact that I smile so often and bubble over with authentic joy on most days is not a coincidence, it is a gift from God.

Since Mom and Dad died, I've held my joy as a gift and offered it to those I've encountered. The idea that I serve a God who doesn't only give me joy, but refreshes my joy morning after morning blows my mind. In my grieving process, I met the God who gives, the God who takes away and the God who restores. Yet, I've also met the God of joy; the God of a joy that bubbles over; the God of a contagious joy that I just can't keep to myself. Perhaps this is the joy referenced by Jeremiah in Lamentations 3:22-23 when he said, "Because of the Lord's great love we are not consumed, for His compassions never fail. They are new every morning; great is your faithfulness."

CHAPTER 16:

In Memory

There are days, even months, when I don't cry about my parents. They are on my mind daily, but not necessarily in sad ways. Their presence is felt in the crease of my smile when I've laughed really hard and in the deep breath that accompanies a long day. When I need an encouraging word, I vividly remember words from Mom and when I need a chuckle, I think of Dad saying something in his mountain twang.

It is because of the length of time that I go without outwardly mourning, that I am so thrown off when emotions surface. Case and point, writing out my wedding program. I literally sat for hours with warm tears sitting in my eyes as I contemplated what to put in the area of "Parents of the Bride." I know it's not proper etiquette to write the name of a deceased parent on that part of the program, yet I hold in tension the huge role they've played in my big day.

For every bridal dress fitting, I imagined Mom marveling over the beauty of the dress; I thought about the huge smile that would have been on Dad's face at the "First Look" photos. Every day I longed for "Good Morning" calls I would have gotten from Mommy reminding me of the countdown; and I thought of how annoyed I would have been at Dad for constantly reminding me of how much he was going to miss me, even though I was living closer to him than I had in years (lol).

In all honesty, my parents have been the depth of my thoughts and the very present peace in my matriculation of my entire wedding planning process. Yet, etiquette told me to omit their names or put them in an "In Memory" section; society told me to do what I wanted. But in all actuality, all I *wanted* is for my mommy to tell me exactly what to do; I *wanted* her to fill in the blank and tell me what to write in the section under "Bridal Party" where I was supposed to list the "Parents of the Bride."

You see I go days, even months, without crying over my parents. But every now and then I have one of those days where I don't want them "In Memory"- I want them right here with me in the present. On those days when I want them closest or I begin to feel as if my parents not being here is unfair, I remember a phrase used by Mom so often, "The Lord gives and the Lord takes away." It's a phrase Mom used so often following a tragic house fire back in 2014.

On June 1, 2014 at approximately 9:00pm I stood outside my family's Chapel Hill home watching it burn to the ground in a fire. I remember feeling helpless; hopeless. Four days later I stood with Mom beside my beloved grandmother's bed singing the old gospel hymn "When I Lay My Burdens Down" as she took her last breath at the age of 100. In four short days, my family experienced traumatic loss and I was left with an array of unanswered questions for God.

The morning after the fire, Mom wanted to go back to the place where our beautiful brick home once stood. As Dad scaled the premises, I began pouring my confusion out to Mom. "Mommy," I began, "I can't believe this happened. It just doesn't seem fair. How could God allow this to happen?" With raised eyebrows and a soft smile, Mommy said, "Kiya, the Lord gives and the Lord takes away. This fire may have taken our home, but it did not touch our souls." It was that reminder that got us through the days and weeks that followed; the reminder that the God who'd provided the house 24 years earlier was the same God who would provide in the days, weeks, months and years to come; the reminder that we were no further from God simply because things didn't *seem* fair or weren't going our way. God was still very much with our family; God was still very much in control.

In the wake of my parents' death, much of their rich wisdom resurfaced in my mind. Quotes, questions and challenges from my parents are among the headlines of my everyday thoughts. As I navigate my "new normal" and go deeper in my relationship with God, I am comforted by the truth that "The Lord Gives and the Lord Takes Away."

In my mind, God's love for me was [mostly] reflected in what He gave me: peace of mind, joy, a loving family, prosperous friendships, health, opportunities, spiritual gifts and talents. Yet, in the wake of losing my parents, I was faced with a very real question: How do I experience love from God in the face of loss, agony, disappointment, abandonment and defeat? God answered this question by reminding me that I was making Him far too *small* if I only thought His love functioned in the realm of "giving." God expanded this explanation by showing me a different kind of love...the kind of Godly love that didn't just give, but that also took away. God showed me that His love was not predicated or gauged on my trial, for there was nothing I could do to make God love me anymore or any less than He already did. God was not punishing me by taking my parents; instead, God was taking me on a journey to discover true covenant relationship with Him.

Through this journey, I met a God who's never left me; a God who wipes my tears and holds me tight; a God who sustains and maintains me on every step of this journey; a God who raises up both the expected and unexpected to provide provision and comfort; a God who understands my language when my pain takes away my words; a God who provides wisdom and insight when I don't know which way to turn. This journey has taken me deeper in my faith as I've come to embrace the truth that "the Lord gives and the Lord takes away" (Job 1:21).

CHAPTER 17:

An Open Letter to Mommy and Daddy

Dear Mommy & Daddy,

*A*s the hot North Carolina summer beats on my sun kissed skin, I am left pondering my process and progress of the last three years. My daily thoughts of you leave a sweet dew on my mind that delights even my most challenging days. For my joy comes not in the loss of you, but in the faithfulness of God. Mommy, after you died, I didn't think I could make it a single day. Daddy, I felt my world shutting down when you died. Your deaths challenged, strained, pushed and motivated me. Yet, despite the arduous seasons of grief and turmoil, I am here. I am still standing, more grounded in my faith than ever; more excited than ever to share the Gospel of a God who gives, takes away and restores. For 28 years, I knew the God who gave, thus *abruptly meeting the God who "takes away" was an unwelcomed (and at times an unbearable) feat. Yet, through it all, God never failed me. He never left me alone. My understanding of your death has been informed by my love for a God who gave, took away and is restoring me; my understanding of your death has informed my entire theology.*

Anyone can worship a God who gives; a God who so quickly answers prayers. Yet, there is a deeper relationship that is cultivated when one finds Holy Hands amidst Hellish seasons, worship despite worry and praying lips in loneliness. In the past three years, I've found that Lily in the Valley that Mama and Papa used to sing about; I've found that love truly lifts me; and I know for a fact that there is power in the blood of Jesus. You spent your lives bringing me to Jesus, yet it was in your deaths that I truly met Him for myself. Through your lives, my life is better. Through your deaths, my life has been transformed.

Thank you and I will love you forever.

Kiya

Acknowledgements

To my beloved family and loving friends who pushed me to complete this awesome task, I am so grateful for you.

A special thanks to everyone on the KWS Ministries Team who helped to make this dream a reality. To Vanessa, the ever-efficient Editor, you are amazing. To Kevin, the brains behind my marketing, you are the best. To Eric, the greatest Sound Engineer in the world, thank you!

To my incredible readers, I APPRECIATE YOU! If you were blessed by this book, I want you to share it with someone and remember to write an online review to encourage others purchase this book. Also, feel free to drop me a line via email to tell me about your embrace of grace or simply to share your thoughts on this book. You can reach me directly at Kiya@KiyaWardShears.com.

If you would like to read more of my work, attend one of my events, book me for a speaking engagement or stay connected, be sure to check out my website at www.KiyaWardShears.com.

Made in the USA
Monee, IL
09 May 2021